SWEET LITTLE BABY

Lullaby Prayer Book   for God's Greatest Gift

Written and sung by Trinice L. Cunningham

Illustrated by Haley Nicely

Instrumental Music and Recording by Rob McCrady

HIGH BRIDGE
BOOKS & MEDIA

Below are QR codes to the lullaby, both with vocals and as an instrumental. In the back of the book, you'll find a place to keep record of all your baby's sweet little moments.

With Vocals

Instrumental
Guitar Strumming

DEDICATION

This lullaby prayer book is inspired by my Lord Jesus Christ and dedicated to our grandson, Hank Barrett Freeman.

Also, to every baby that is a gift from our Creator God who lives in Heaven or on Earth.

He formed each one of us in our mother's wombs, and He knew us before we were born.

You made all the delicate, inner parts of my body
and knit me together in my mother's womb.
Thank you for making me so wonderfully complex!
Your workmanship is marvelous—how well I know it.
You watched me as I was being formed in utter seclusion,
as I was woven together in the dark of the womb.
You saw me before I was born.
Every day of my life was recorded in your book.
Every moment was laid out
before a single day had passed.
How precious are your thoughts about me, O God.
They cannot be numbered!

—PSALM 139:13–17 NLT

THANK YOU!

I need to first thank the man God gave me to always be my knight in shining armor, my life partner, and my champion husband, Terry Lee Cunningham. You have always been my biggest supporter in anything I have ever wanted to do, and I love you to infinity and beyond.

Also, to those of you in my immediate and extended family and my many friends with whom I have shared my silly songs and rhymes, your encouragement meant more than you know.

Finally, thank you doesn't seem enough to the amazingly gifted people God put in my life to help make His dream come true for me.

My prayer has always been to God be all the glory and honor.

Sweet little baby,
don't you cry.
You are the apple
of God's eye.

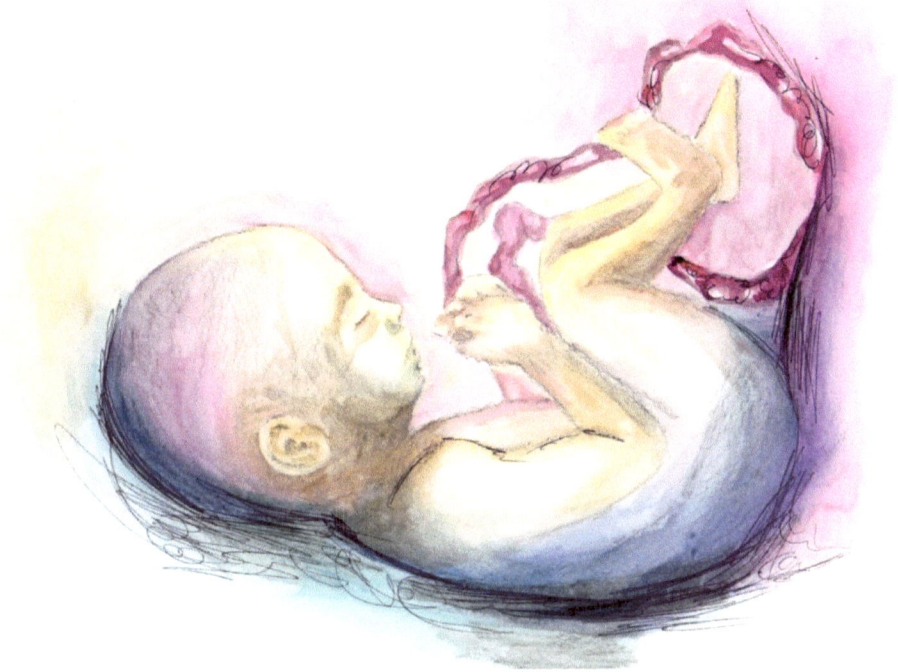

Keep me as the apple of Your eye;
Hide me under the shadow of Your wings …

PSALM 17:8 NKJV

He is the one that
you should know,
will protect you
as you grow.

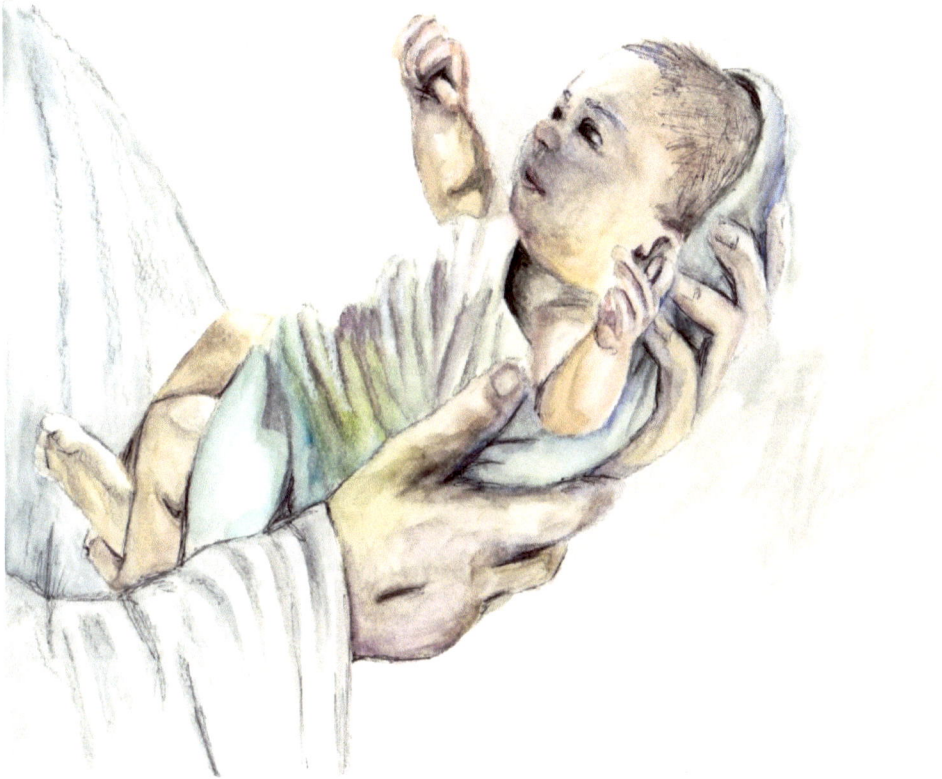

Do not fear, for I am with you;
do not be afraid, for I am your God.
I will strengthen you; I will help you;
I will hold on to you with My righteous right hand.

ISAIAH 41:10 HCSB

You are precious
in His sight.
He sent Jesus
to be your light.

When Jesus spoke again to the people, he said,
"I am the light of the world.
Whoever follows me will never walk in darkness,
but will have the light of life."

JOHN 8:12 NIV

He has a plan for
your good life,
not to harm you
or cause you strife.

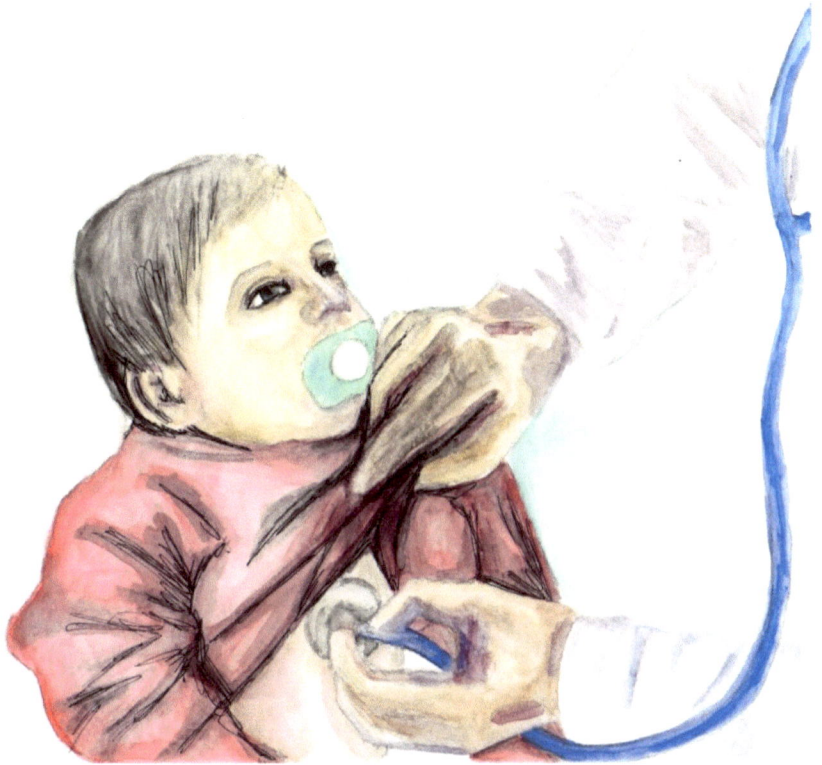

"For I know the plans I have for you," declares the Lord,
"plans to prosper you and not to harm you,
plans to give you hope and a future."

Jeremiah 29:11 NIV

He wants you
to invite Him in.
Then He will help
you with your sin.

If you declare with your mouth, "*Jesus is Lord*," and believe in your heart that God raised him from the dead, you will be saved.

ROMANS 10:9 NIV, EMPHASIS ADDED

As you get bigger
and learn His ways, He
will be with you
all of your days.

My child, never forget the things I have taught you.
Store my commands in your heart.
If you do this, you will live many years,
and your life will be satisfying.

PROVERBS 3:1-2 NLT

Then His Light will
shine all around, and
you'll be the sweetest
little baby in town.

For this is how God loved the world:
He gave his one and only Son,
so that everyone who believes in him will not
perish but have eternal life.

JOHN 3:16 NLT

Sweet Little Moments to Remember

_____

_____

_____

_____

_____

_____

_____

_____

_____

_____

_____

Sweet Little Moments to Remember

Sweet Little Moments to Remember

Sweet Little Moments to Remember

_____

_____

_____

_____

_____

_____

_____

_____

_____

_____

_____

_____

_____

Sweet Little Moments to Remember

_____

_____

_____

_____

_____

_____

_____

_____

_____

_____

_____

Sweet Little Moments to Remember

Sweet Little Moments to Remember

Hey everyone, I'm **Trinice Lynn Cunningham**, better known as Trini but most honored to be called Grammy. I was born and raised in Southeastern Ohio for the first thirty years of my life, and I now live in East Tennessee with my husband, Terry, whom the Lord allowed me to have, hold, and cherish in April of 1986 until eternity in heaven. We have four beautiful adult daughters, and this book idea began when our middle daughter, Amy, was pregnant with our grandson, Hank.

The Lord woke me up at 3:00 a.m. to the memory of my dad singing the song "Hush Little Baby" over me. As I thought about the words to that song, it dawned on me that when we get **things** and those **things** break and we get **more things,** we don't become the sweetest little babies in town. That actually makes us discontent, greedy, and selfish. Jesus is the only gift we can receive from our Heavenly Father that will make us the sweetest little babies in town. So as you say or sing these words over your babies who are a gift from God, my prayer is that they receive it into their tiny spirit and God's peace that passes all understanding will comfort them as they grow to know Jesus Christ as Lord and Savior of their life.

To God be all glory, honor, and praise! In *Jesus'* name, amen!

www.ingramcontent.com/pod-product-compliance
Lightning Source LLC
LaVergne TN
LVHW072135070426
835513LV00003B/112

9 781962 802048